PRESENTED TO

_____

BY

_____

DATE

_____

TEAMWORK
MAKES THE
DREAM
WORK

JOHN C. MAXWELL

J. COUNTRYMAN
NASHVILLE, TENNESSEE
WWW.JCOUNTRYMAN.COM

ACKNOWLEDGEMENTS

Grateful permission is made to Thomas Nelson Publishers for permission to reprint from the following books:

Maxwell, John C. 1999.
The 21 Indispensible Qualities of a Leader: Becoming the Person Others Will Want to Follow.
Nashville, Tennessee: Thomas Nelson Publishers.

Maxwell, John C. 2001.
The 17 Indisputable Laws of Teamwork: Embrace Them and Empower Your Team.
Nashville, Tennessee: Thomas Nelson Publishers.

Maxwell, John C. 1997.
Becoming a Person of Influence.
Nashville, Tennessee: Thomas Nelson Publishers.

Unless otherwise indicated, all Scripture quotations in this book are from the New King James Version (NKJV) ©1979, 1980, 1982, 1992, Thomas Nelson, Inc., Publisher.

Designed by Kirk DouPonce, UDG|DesignWorks, Sisters, Oregon

Project editor: Kathy Baker

ISBN 0-8499-5508-4

Published in association with Sealy M. Yates, Literary Agent, Orange, California.

Printed and bound in Belgium

www.thomasnelson.com

Are you dreaming big enough? That may strike you as a funny question. "Dream bigger?" you may ask. "I'm not accomplishing the little goals I have," you may say, "and you want me to dream about doing bigger things?"

I find that many people are afraid to dream big. They are reluctant to hope for too much because they don't want to be disappointed. As a result, they satisfy themselves with the mundane.

It doesn't have to be that way. Even if you suspect in your heart of hearts that you don't have the talent or resources to accomplish your goals—much less accomplish your wildest dreams—you don't have to give them up. You just need to change your strategy. Instead of working alone, you need to be part of a team. Here is what a team can do for you:

+ It makes you better than you are.
+ It multiplies your value to others.
+ It enables you to do what you do best.
+ It allows you to help others do their best.
+ It gives you more time.
+ It provides you with companionship.
+ It helps you fulfill the desires of your heart.
+ It makes everyone on the team a winner.

Teams are incredible things. No task is too great, no accomplishment too grand, no dream too far-fetched for a team. It takes teamwork to make the dream work.

It Takes a Team

COMING TOGETHER IS A BEGINNING.

KEEPING TOGETHER IS PROGRESS.

WORKING TOGETHER IS SUCCESS.

—JOHN C. MAXWELL

Teams come in all shapes and sizes.
If you're married, you and your spouse
are a team. If you are employed by
an organization, you and your colleagues
are a team. If you volunteer your time,
you and your fellow workers are a team.
As Dan Devine joked, "A team is a team
is a team. Shakespeare said that many times."
While the great playwright may not have
said exactly that, the concept is nonetheless
true. Every day in some way, you are
a part of a team. The question is not,
"Will you participate in something that
involves others?" The question is, "Will your
involvement with others be successful?"

— *THE 17 INDISPUTABLE LAWS OF TEAMWORK*

No problem is insurmountable.

With a little courage,

teamwork, and determination

a person can overcome anything.

— B. DODGE

I n 1935, twenty-one-year-old Tenzing Norgay made his first trip to Mount Everest. He worked as a porter for a British team of mountaineers. A Sherpa born in the high altitudes of Nepal, Tenzing had been drawn to the mountain from the time that westerners began visiting the area with the dream of climbing to the mountain's peak. The first group had come in 1920. Fifteen years later, climbers were still trying to figure out how to conquer the mountain.

The farthest Tenzing's first expedition would go was up to the North Col, which was at an altitude of 22,000 feet. (A col is a flat area along a mountain's ridge between peaks.) And it was just below that col that the climbing party made a gruesome discovery. They came across a wind-shredded tent, and in that tent was a skeleton with a little frozen skin stretched over the bones. It was sitting in an odd position, with one boot off and the laces of the remaining boot between its bony fingers.

HARSHEST PLACE ON THE PLANET

Mountain climbing is not for the faint of heart because the world's highest peaks are some of the most inhospitable places on earth. Everest is remote. At 29,035 feet, the altitude incapacitates all but the hardiest and most experienced climbers, and the weather is ruthlessly unforgiving. Experts believe that the bodies of about 120 failed climbers remain on the mountain today.[1]

The body Tenzing and the others found in 1935 was that of Maurice Wilson, an Englishman who had sneaked into Tibet and tried to climb the mountain without the permission of the Tibetan government. Because he was trying to make the ascent quietly, he had hired only three porters to climb the mountain with him. As they approached the North Col, those men had refused to go any farther with him. Wilson decided to try to make the climb on his own. That decision killed him.

Only someone who has climbed a great mountain knows what it takes to make it to the top. For thirty-two years, between 1920 and 1952, seven major expeditions tried—and failed—to make it to the top of Everest. Tenzing Norgay was on six of those expeditions. His fellow climbers joked that he had a third lung because of his ability to climb tirelessly while carrying heavy loads. During those climbs, he earned everyone's respect.

NOT A CASUAL STROLL

In 1953, Tenzing embarked on his seventh expedition to Everest with a British group led by Colonel John Hunt. By then, he was respected not only as a porter who could carry heavy loads at high altitudes, but also as a mountaineer and full-fledged expedition member, an honor unusual for a Sherpa. The year before he had climbed to a height of 28,250 feet with a Swiss team. At that time, it was the closest any human being had come to the top of Everest.

Tenzing was also engaged to be the British group's sirdar for the trip, the Sherpa leader who would hire, organize, and lead the porters for the journey. That was no small task. To get just two people from base camp up to the summit, the team brought ten high-altitude climbers, including a New Zealander named Edmund Hillary. Altogether, the men would require two and a half tons of equipment and food. Those supplies couldn't be trucked or airlifted to the base of the mountain. They would have to be delivered to Kathmandu, then carried on the backs of men and women 180 miles up and down Himalayan ridges and over rivers crossed by narrow rope-and-plank bridges to the base camp. Tenzing would have to hire between two hundred and three hundred people just to get the supplies to the mountain.

Supplies that would be needed by the party above the base camp would have to be carried up the mountain by another forty porters, each a Sherpa with extensive mountain experience. The best third of that team would continue working higher up the mountain, carrying up the seven hundred fifty pounds of necessary equipment in thirty-pound loads. Only Tenzing and three other porters would have the strength and skill to go to the high camps near the summit.

IT TAKES A TEAM

For each level that the climbers reached, a higher degree of teamwork was required. One set of men would exhaust themselves just to get equipment up the mountain for the next group. Two-man teams would work their way up the mountain, finding a path, cutting steps, securing ropes. And then they would be done, having spent themselves to make the next leg of the climb possible for another team. Of the teamwork involved, Tenzing remarked, "You do not climb a mountain like Everest by trying to race ahead on your own, or by competing with your comrades. You do it slowly and carefully, by unselfish teamwork. Certainly I wanted to reach the top myself; it was the thing I had dreamed of all my life. But if the lot fell to some one else I would take it like a man, and not a cry-baby. For that is the mountain way."[2]

The team of climbers, using the "mountain way," ultimately made it possible for two pairs to make their attempts at reaching the summit. The first was Tom Bourdillon and Charles Evans. When they tried and failed, it was time for the second team—Tenzing and Edmund. Tenzing wrote of the first team,

> They were worn-out, sick with exhaustion, and, of course, terribly disappointed that they had not reached the summit themselves. But still . . . they did everything they could to advise and help us. And I thought, yes, that is how it is on a mountain. That is how a mountain makes

men great. For where would Hillary and I have been without the others? Without the climbers who had made the route and the Sherpas who had carried the loads? Without Bourdillon and Evans, Hunt and Da Namgyal, who had cleared the way ahead? Without Lowe and Gregory, Ang Hyima, Ang Tempra, and Penba, who were there only to help us? It was only because of the work and sacrifice of all of them that we were now to have our chance at the top.[3]

They made the most of their chance. On May 29, 1953, Tenzing Norgay and Edmund Hillary accomplished what no other human being ever had: They stood on the summit of Mount Everest, the world's highest peak!

Could Tenzing and Hillary have made it alone? The answer is no. Could they have made it without a great team? Again, the answer is no. Why? Because it takes teamwork to make the dream work. If you want to climb a great mountain, you cannot do it alone.

— *THE 17 INDISPUTABLE LAWS OF TEAMWORK*

Teamwork gives you the best opportunity

to turn vision into reality.

— JOHN C. MAXWELL

HOW TO "C" YOUR WAY INTO BETTER TEAMWORK

It takes a team to achieve a dream. But what does it take to create a team?

Commitment that inspires results

Contributions that make a difference

Competency that raises the standard

Communication that increases effectiveness

Cooperation that creates harmony

Chemistry that enhances personal connection

Creativity that enlarges the team's potential

Conflict management that reduces tension rapidly

Cohesiveness that allows change to be rapid

Community that makes the journey fun

If your team can seize these C's, then you will be able to see your way to victory.

O n November 20, 1988, the *Los Angeles Times* reported the following incident:

A screaming woman, trapped in a car dangling from a freeway transition road in East Los Angeles was rescued Saturday morning. The nineteen-year-old woman apparently fell asleep behind the wheel at a quarter after midnight. The car, which plunged through a guard rail, was left dangling by its left rear wheel. A half dozen passing motorists stopped, grabbed some ropes from one of their vehicles, tied the ropes to the back of the woman's car, and hung on until the emergency units arrived. A ladder was extended from below to help stabilize the car while firefighters tied the vehicle to two trucks with cables and chains.

"Every time we would move the car," said one of the rescuers, "she'd yell and scream. She was in pain."

It took almost two and one-half hours for the passers-by, highway patrol officers, tow truck drivers, and firefighters—about twenty-five people in all—to secure the car and pull the woman to safety.

"It was kinda funny," Los Angeles County Fire Capt. Ross Marshall recalled later. "She kept saying, 'I'll do it myself.'"[4]

*It marks a big step in your
development when you come to realize
that other people can help you
do a better job than you could do alone.*

— ANDREW CARNEGIE

*Alone we can do so little;
together we can do so much.*

— HELEN KELLER

*No one can whistle a symphony.
It takes an orchestra to play it.*

— HALFORD E. LUCCOCK

N

obody is more keenly aware of the importance of teamwork than a combat pilot. Take for example Charlie Plumb.

Every pilot is acutely aware of the team effort required to put a jet in the air. It takes hundreds of people utilizing dozens of technical specialties to launch, monitor, support, land, and maintain an aircraft. Even more people are involved if that plane is armed for combat. Charlie Plumb, an Annapolis graduate who served in Vietnam in the mid-sixties and eventually retired as a captain, was undoubtedly aware that many people worked tirelessly to keep him flying. But despite the efforts of the best-trained air support group in the world, Plumb found himself in a North Vietnamese prison as a POW after his F-4 Phantom jet was shot down May 19, 1967, during his seventy-fifth mission.

Plumb was held prisoner for nearly six grueling years, part of the time in the infamous Hanoi Hilton. During those years he and his fellow prisoners were humiliated, starved, tortured, and forced to live in squalid conditions. Yet he didn't let the experience break him. He now says, "Our unity through our faith in God and in our love for country were the great strength which kept us going through some very difficult times."

Plumb was released from his imprisonment on February 18, 1973, and continued his career in the Navy. But an incident years after his return to the United States marked his life as surely as his imprisonment. One day he and his wife, Cathy, were eating in a restaurant when a man came to the table and said, "You're Plumb. You flew jet fighters in Vietnam."

"That's right," answered Plumb, "I did."

"It was fighter squadron 114 on the *Kitty Hawk*. You were shot down. You were parachuted into enemy hands," the man continued. "You spent six years as a prisoner of war."

The former pilot was taken back. He looked at the man, trying to identify him, but couldn't. "How in the world did you know that?" Plumb finally asked.

"I packed your parachute."

Plumb was staggered. All he could do was struggle to his feet and shake the man's hand. "I must tell you," Plumb finally said, "I've said a lot of prayers of thanks for your nimble fingers, but I didn't realize I'd have the opportunity of saying thanks in person."

Today, Charlie Plumb is a motivational speaker to Fortune 500 companies, government agencies, and other organizations. He often tells the story of the man who packed his parachute, and he uses it to deliver a message on teamwork. He says, "In a world where downsizing forces us to do more with less, we must empower the team. 'Packing others' parachutes' can mean the difference in survival. Yours and your team's!"

— *THE 17 INDISPUTABLE LAWS OF TEAMWORK*

*One person seeking glory
doesn't accomplish much. Success is
the result of people pulling together
to meet common goals.*

—JOHN C. MAXWELL

Alex Haley, the author of *Roots*, had a picture in his office, showing a turtle sitting atop a fence. The picture is there to remind him of a lesson he learned long ago: "If you see a turtle on a fence post, you know he had some help."

Said Alex, "Any time I start thinking, Wow, isn't this marvelous what I've done! I look up at that picture and remember how this turtle—me—got up on that post."

— PHILIP BARRY OSBORNE
THE HANDBOOK OF MAGAZINE ARTICLE WRITING

If a team is to reach its potential, each player must be willing to subordinate his personal goals to the good of the team.

— BUD WILKINSON
THE BOOK OF FOOTBALL WISDOM

We must learn to live together as brothers
or perish together as fools.

— MARTIN LUTHER KING, JR.

One man can be a crucial ingredient on a team,
but one man cannot make a team.

— KAREEM ABDUL-JABBAR

Personal Sacrifice

THE FREEDOM TO DO YOUR OWN THING
ENDS WHEN YOU HAVE OBLIGATIONS
AND RESPONSIBILITIES. IF YOU WANT
TO FAIL YOURSELF—YOU CAN—
BUT YOU CANNOT DO YOUR
OWN THING IF YOU HAVE
RESPONSIBILITIES TO
TEAM MEMBERS.

—LOU HOLTZ

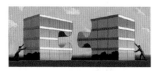

My basic principle is that
you don't make decisions because they are easy,
you don't make them because they're cheap,
you don't make them because they're popular;
you make them because they're right.

— THEODORE HESBURGH

Jimmy Townsend once remarked,
"Anybody who can still do at sixty
what he was doing at twenty
wasn't doing much at twenty."
That's true — if you work alone.
You see, the bad news is that people
don't have the energy to do more
personally at sixty than at twenty.
The good news is that if you're part of
a team, you can do more collectively
at sixty than you could at twenty.

— JOHN C. MAXWELL

I n his autobiography, *Just As I Am,* Billy Graham acknowledges that his ministry and all that he has accomplished over the years have come with the help of the people who have partnered with him. He says,

> As I reflect back over half a century, I realize more than ever that this ministry has been a team effort. Without the help of others—our supporters, our prayer partners, our Team and staff, and our board of directors—the ministry would not have been possible. Lord Nelson, the British naval commander . . . once said (following Shakespeare) that it had been his happiness to command a band of brothers. He knew he had not gained victories alone. That also has been one of our secrets.[5]

For more than half a century, one of the key people on that team was Billy Graham's friend T. W. Wilson. As a youth, Graham knew Wilson, whom he described as a big man and a bit of a rough customer, someone who could have been a bouncer. But as a young man Wilson became a Christian, trained for the ministry, and then became an effective evangelist.

In 1948, as Graham's ministry and responsibilities were rapidly expanding, he asked Wilson to work with him. At first, his boyhood friend resisted, but Graham was persistent. "God has spoken to me that you are to come with me and help me," Graham told him. "I need somebody who is an evangelist; I need somebody who knows me and my ministry, my family; I need somebody I can trust."

"I didn't want to come with Billy," Wilson later recalled.[6] After all, Wilson had his own successful ministry and was holding city-wide crusades himself. But he ultimately made the decision to follow Graham. He set aside his own dreams of ministry in order to help Graham with his.

That decision made a huge difference, not only in their lives, but also in the lives of all the people they reached together until Wilson's death in 2001.

Sometimes you have to sacrifice a small dream of your own in order to accomplish a bigger dream with someone else. It takes a courageous and humble person to make such a decision. But look at what can result. Only heaven can measure the impact of Billy Graham's ministry. And what was Wilson's take on his decision? He stated simply, "I have never regretted it."

A man asked his neighbor
if he could borrow his lawn mower.
The neighbor replied, "I can't because
Ethel is cooking cabbage."

Confused, the man said,
"What does Ethel cooking cabbage
have to do with it?"

"Nothing," the neighbor explained,
"but when you don't want to do something
one excuse is as good as another!"

Remember that the next time you're
tempted to tell others why you can't
do your part on the team.

— LOWELL WALDEN

Winning is often a battle, and there are times in the life of every team player when he or she needs to fight. But if you fight all the time, you can wear yourself out. That's why it's important to pick your battles.

To gain a better perspective of when to fight back and when to sacrifice yourself, practice the following disciplines:

1. Spend Time with People Who Are Different from You. That helps you to appreciate and understand how others think and work. You will be less likely to judge or battle others.

2. In Matters of Personal Preference or Taste, Give In. Keep the main things the main thing. If you don't save yourself for what really matters, you'll wear yourself out and wear out your welcome with others.

3. Don't Take Things Too Personally. Always remember, hurting people hurt people. They are also easily hurt by others.

4. Practice the 101 Percent Principle. Whenever possible, find the 1 percent you do agree on in a difficult situation, and give it 100 percent of your effort.

5. Be a Servant Leader. If your mindset is to serve rather than be served, you will likely encounter less conflict.

T he year 1777 was not a particularly successful one for General Washington and his troops. Following defeats at Brandywine, Paoli, and Germantown and the loss of Philadelphia to the British, Washington and eleven thousand soldiers straggled into Valley Forge on December 19 of that year. The troops were demoralized, and they were facing the prospect of a bitter winter with minimal shelter and comforts.

What those men probably wanted most was to go home and forget about the war for freedom. But if they did, the cost would be high. Positioned as they were, they could keep an eye on the British troops under General Howe in Philadelphia. More importantly, they were in a place where they could defend York, Pennsylvania, to which the Continental Congress had fled when the capital fell to the British. If the men at Valley Forge didn't pay the price, the government would fall, the army would be disbanded, and the Revolutionary War would be lost.

Conditions were horrible. The men were ill-equipped and poorly supplied. A few days after their arrival, Washington wrote to the Continental Congress saying, "2,898 men were unfit for duty because they were barefoot or otherwise naked [insufficiently clothed for the harsh weather]." Things were so bad that sentries had to stand on their hats to ward off frostbite in their feet. By February 1, only 5,000 men were available for service.

Miraculously, the troops didn't give up. They bore the brunt of the difficult winter. But they did more than just hang on and survive. They took the time they had to become better soldiers. Prior to their time at Valley Forge, they were disorganized and untrained. To remedy that, General Washington employed the talents of a former officer in the Prussian army, Baron von Steuben.

First, von Steuben imposed organization on the camp and introduced improved sanitation. Then under his instruction, one company of men was transformed into a crack team of soldiers. They in turn helped to train the other companies of men. Von Steuben also standardized the military maneuvers throughout the army so that the men could work better as a team, no matter which officers commanded them. By the time the army mobilized in June of 1778, they were a match for any group of soldiers, even the British who were considered by some to be the best in the world.

Washington's army went on to win battles against a British army with far superior numbers. And they fought in the battle of Yorktown, the decisive battle that turned the war in favor of the newly formed country. Those of us who live in the United States are grateful to them, for the price they paid more than two hundred years ago paved the way for us to live in a country of great freedom and opportunity. While it's true that the team fails to reach its potential when it fails to pay the price, it's also true that when the price is paid, the rewards can be great. That's the blessing of the Law of the Price Tag

— *The 17 Indisputable Laws of Teamwork*

There are plenty of teams in every
sport that have great players and never
win titles. Most of the time, those players
aren't willing to sacrifice for the greater
good of the team. The funny thing is,
in the end, their unwillingness to sacrifice
only makes individual goals more
difficult to achieve. One thing I believe
to the fullest is that if you think and
achieve as a team, the individual
accolades will take care of themselves
Talent wins games but teamwork
and intelligence win championships.

— MICHAEL JORDAN
I CAN'T ACCEPT NOT TRYING

A SPECIAL RACE

A few years ago in Seattle, Washington, nine finalists were poised at the starting line of a 400 meter race, each planning to do his best and hoping to win the medal for first place.

As the gun went off, the racers sprinted toward the finish line. But one of the runners fell down. He quickly got up and gave his all to catch up with the others. But once again, he fell. His frustration totally overcame him, and he burst into tears and began to sob loudly.

Then a strange thing happened. The rest of the field heard his cries, and they turned to see that he was lying on the track. The runners began to slow down, and then one by one, they stopped, turned around, and went back to him. They picked him up, consoled him, and then together, all nine of them finished the race. In a race made for individual glory, the racers had made themselves into a team.

Where in the world could something like this happen? At the Special Olympics. Perhaps that is why they are called "special!"

T he little old couple walked into McDonald's on a cold winter evening. They looked out of place amid the young families and couples eating there that night. The woman hung on her husband's arm, and he looked at her lovingly. People could tell they had been together a long time.

The old man walked up to the cash register, placed his order and then paid for their meal. The couple took a table near the back and started taking food off of the tray. There was one hamburger, one order of French fries, and a drink.

People began to watch as the man unwrapped the plain hamburger and carefully cut it in half. He placed one half in front of his wife. Then he carefully counted out the French fries, divided them in two piles and neatly placed one pile in front of his wife. He took a sip of the drink, his wife took a sip and then set the cup between them.

As the man began to eat his few bites of hamburger, everyone in McDonald's began to get restless. You knew what they were thinking, "That poor old couple. All they can afford is one meal for the two of them."

A young man stood and came over to the old couple's table. He politely offered to buy another meal for the couple to eat.

The old man replied that they were just fine. They were used to sharing everything.

Then the crowd noticed that the old woman hadn't eaten a bite. She just sat there watching her husband eat and occasionally taking turns sipping the drink. Again the young man came over and begged them to let him buy them something to eat. This time the woman explained that no, they shared everything.

As the old man finished eating and was wiping his face neatly with a napkin the young man could stand it no longer. Again he came over to their table and offered to buy some food. After being politely refused again he finally asked the old woman, "Ma'am, Why aren't you eating? You said that you shared everything. What is it that you are waiting for?"

She answered simply, "The teeth."

Team sports are really difficult things. Sometimes your team wins because of you, sometimes in spite of you and sometimes it's like you're not even there. That's the reality of the team game. Then at one point in my career . . . something wonderful happened, I don't know why or how . . . but I came to understand what "team" meant. It meant that although I didn't get a hit or make a great defensive play, I could impact the team in an incredible and consistent way. I learned I could impact my team by caring first and foremost about the team's success and not my own. I don't mean by rooting for us like a typical fan. Fans are fickle. I mean CARE, really care about the team . . . about "us." I became less selfish, less lazy, less sensitive to negative comments. When I gave up me, I became more. I became a captain, a leader, a better person and I came to understand that life is a team game . . . And you know what? . . . I've found most people aren't team players. They don't realize that life is the only game in town. Someone should tell them. It has made all the difference in the world to me.

— DON MATTINGLY

Working Together

TEAM:

TOGETHER

EVERYONE

ACHIEVES

MORE

—JOHN C. MAXWELL

United States track star Wilma Rudolph, winner of three gold medals in the 1960 Rome Olympics, was asked which medal was her favorite. "My favorite gold medal?" she responded. "That's an easy question. It was the relay, because I won that with my Tennessee State Tigerbelle teammates, and we could celebrate together."

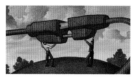

We have not come to compete

with one another. We have come to

complete one another.

— BILL MCCARTNEY

SPOKEN AT PROMISE KEEPERS

It's not how heavy the load,

it's how you carry it.

— JOHN C. MAXWELL

We don't work for each other;

we work with each other.

— STANLEY C. GAULT

If you can laugh together,

you can work together.

— ROBERT ORBEN

L ook at hundreds of winning teams, and you will find that their players have four things in common:

1. THEY PLAY TO WIN:

The difference between playing to win and playing not to lose is often the difference between success and mediocrity.

2. THEY HAVE A WINNING ATTITUDE:

Team members believe in themselves, their teammates, and their dream. And they don't allow negative thinking to derail them.

3. THEY KEEP IMPROVING:

The highest reward for their efforts isn't what they get from it, but who they become because of it. Team members know intuitively that if they're through improving, they're through.

4. THEY MAKE THEIR TEAMMATES MORE SUCCESSFUL:

Winners are empowerers. As Charlie Brower says, "Few people are successful unless a lot of other people want them to be."

Two are better than one,

Because they have a good reward

for their labor. For if they fall,

one will lift up his companion.

But woe to him who is alone when he falls,

For he has no one to help him up.

Again, if two lie down together,

they will keep warm;

But how can one be warm alone?

Though one may be overpowered

by another, two can withstand him.

And a threefold cord is not quickly broken.

— ECCLESIASTES 4:9–12

Vision, policies, and plans are more or less
useless unless they are known to all
who may be concerned with them.
Lord Montgomery, commander of the Eighth Army,
made it a rule that the plan of the campaign
should be made known to every soldier.

— FRED SMITH
LEARNING TO LEAD

S uccessful teams are ones whose members say yes—to big dreams, to great challenges, and to each other. Take a look at the following ten questions. If you and your teammates can say yes to them, then you are well on your way to accomplishing your dream:

1. Do we trust each other?

2. Do we have concern for each other?

3. Do team members feel free to communicate openly?

4. Do we understand our team's goals?

5. Do we have a commitment to those goals?

6. Do we make good use of each member's abilities?

7. Do we handle conflict successfully?

8. Does everyone participate?

9. Do we respect our individual differences?

10. Do we like being members of this team?

Your teammates will

stretch your vision or choke your dream.

—JOHN C. MAXWELL

Will and Charlie grew up working with their dad, who was a doctor, in southeastern Minnesota. "We came along in medicine like farm boys do on a farm," Will once said of their life with their father in the 1870s. They assisted their father with patient visits, and even with autopsies, so it was natural when both boys went to get their medical degrees. Will graduated from the University of Michigan Medical School in 1883 and Charlie from Chicago Medical College in 1888.

After their formal education, they both returned to practice medicine with their father, and they thrived working together. In 1889, as requested by Mother Alfred Moes of the Sisters of St. Francis, the three doctors built the first general hospital in southeastern Minnesota, a facility with twenty-seven beds called Saint Mary's Hospital.

The two men who had learned medicine from boyhood became highly skilled surgeons. In fact, Charlie, the younger of the two, was called a "surgical wonder." He could work in any area of surgery, and he developed groundbreaking procedures, some of which are still in use today. Their skill with patients created a huge demand for their services, so starting in the 1890s, they began inviting other doctors to join them in their practice. Some joined as surgeons, others to develop and run the laboratories, and still others to develop editorial services so that they could share medical discoveries with other physicians.

The brothers' medical skills were great, but their greatest asset was something else—it was their ability to rely on each other and work as a team along with the other doctors they recruited. That sense of teamwork allowed them to pool their resources and abilities for the sake of their patients. Out of that ability and inclination grew a groundbreaking philosophy of medicine. Will explained,

> "It (has become) necessary to develop medicine as a cooperative science; the clinician, the specialist, and the laboratory workers uniting for the good of the patient. Individualism in medicine can no longer exist."

The new style of working together led to medical and organizational breakthroughs. Doctors began to develop medical specialties while others perfected lab techniques. For example, Dr. Louis Wilson developed a rapid way to diagnose surgical specimens so that surgeons could explore, diagnose, and repair all in one operation. Dr. Henry Plummer developed a revolutionary system of keeping records in which all of a patient's information was kept in a single file so that he could be diagnosed and treated more effectively. Plummer also designed the brothers' new medical facility where the medical departments, laboratories, workshops, editorial services, and business office were brought under one roof. It's a testament to Will's sense of teamwork that he once said that the best day's work he ever did for the clinic was hiring Henry Plummer.

The building that Plummer designed and the doctors built was given the name of the founding doctors, Will and Charlie Mayo. In 1919, the brothers turned over all the assets of the Mayo Clinic, along with nearly all of their personal fortune, to a foundation so that the work they began back in the 1880s in Rochester, Minnesota, could be continued.

The organization now includes three clinics and four hospitals in three states. It employs more than twenty-five thousand physicians, scientists, nurses and allied health professionals. More than five million people have been treated at the Mayo Clinic. Today, like in its early days, the organization integrates medical research, education, publishing, and practice. So far, more than thirteen thousand physicians have learned their profession there.

Charlie Mayo once observed, "If we excel in anything, it is our capacity for translating idealism into action." Today, the Mayo Clinic continues to take action by doing creative research, producing medical breakthroughs, training doctors, and even producing Nobel Prize winners, but its greatest contribution is its philosophy of teamwork. Harry Harwick, who worked with Will and Charlie Mayo for thirty-one years, remarked, "The first and perhaps greatest lesson I learned from the Mayos was that of teamwork. For 'my brother and I' was no mere convenient term of reference, but rather the expression of a basic, indivisible philosophy of life."

Their teamwork made their dream work.[7]

When your great players are team players,
everybody else follows their lead.

The best team doesn't always win —
it's usually the team that gets along best.

— JOHN C. MAXWELL

Teammates can learn a lesson from watching how honey bees work together. Bees continually feed one another. The workers feed the helpless queen who cannot feed herself. They feed the drones during their period of usefulness in the hive. And of course they feed the young.

But they also work together to create a healthy environment for the hive. In cold weather, they cluster together for warmth. In the heat of summer, they fan their wings to cool the hive. If they didn't, they wouldn't survive.

When the hive grows to beyond its capacity, it prepares to swarm. Scout bees search for a suitable place for a new colony and then report back to the group by doing an elaborate dance. Then a group of bees sets out on its own with a new queen to establish a new hive. Bees work together, but not just to survive or even thrive. They aren't content until they multiply. We should set no lower standard for ourselves.

Even when you've played the game of your life,

it's the feeling of teamwork that you'll remember

You'll forget the plays, the shots, and the scores,

but you'll never forget your teammates.

— AUTHOR UNKNOWN

Leading the Team

THE TEST OF A LEADER
IS TAKING THE VISION
FROM ME TO WE.

—JOHN C. MAXWELL

The highest compliments
leaders can receive are those that are given
by the people who work for them.

— JAMES L. BARKSDALE

No one of us is more important
than the rest of us.

— RAY KROC

If you want to succeed as a team, you have to be able to turn the key. Here are four keys that will help you to understand how a team can come to achieve its dream. Know that . . .

Personnel determine the **Potential** of the team

Vision determines the **Direction** of the team

Work Ethic determines the **Preparation** of the team

Leadership determines the **Success** of the team

If you recruit good players
and they play well, you're a genius.
So for a year or two you'll be called
a genius. Sometimes a "genius manager"
will recruit bad players who play poorly,
which will make people wonder how
come a genius got so dumb so fast.

— WHITEY HERZOG

People who feel good about themselves

produce good results.

— JOHN C. MAXWELL

In the late 1970s, Bill Walsh took over the leadership of the San Francisco 49ers. Within two years, he turned a team that had been a doormat into a dynasty of NFL champions. Here's his formula:

1. Resist the urge to clean house.

Give yourself time to evaluate existing talent, and give the team time to learn what you're looking for. Those who can supply it will be worth your patience. Those who can't will move on.

2. Seize control from the start.

A committee can't save a sinking ship. Make sure all major decisions go through you.

3. Take inventory of assets and obstacles.

You need to know what hand you've got before you can play. List the team's pluses and minuses, including personnel, attitudes, administration, and perceptions.

4. Find the hidden gems.

Look for raw talent, not just a solid track record. Quarterback Joe Montana was a third-round draft pick, small and inconsistent. But Walsh saw Montana's potential when he rallied Notre Dame to win the 1979 Cotton Bowl. Walsh's theory: One miracle can become a life skill with training, support, and practice.

— ADAPTED FROM *MANAGER'S EDGE*

The greatest destroyer
of a championship team is
a weak person who
should not be on that team.

The term "first string" comes from the sport of archery. In the thirteenth century the longbow was a popular and feared weapon. Most armor was no defense against it. In order to be a good marksman, an archer had to have a good bowstring. His favorite was called his first string. The meaning has changed and is now associated with the best team on the field.

If things get worse,
I will have to ask you
to stop helping me.

—SIGN SEEN ON
A LEADER'S DESK

The first method of estimating the intelligence of a ruler is to look at the men he has around him.

— NICCOLO MACHIAVELLI

GIVE THEM WHAT THEY REALLY WANT

Leading yourself is no easy task. It takes self-discipline, planning, and the opportunity to get the job done. But leading a team is different—and much more difficult. It starts with a better understanding of human nature.

As you lead your team, remember that the people on your team will always want five things from you:

1. Authenticity that enables a solid connection

2. Confidence that empowers and inspires them

3. Awareness and ability to meet people's needs

4. Ability to lead with strategic direction

5. Moments of victory during the journey

If you provide those five things, people will always have good reasons to follow you.

Leadership of a team is the highest expression of servant leadership. This is true because team leadership embodies each of the principles of servant leadership:

1. You must humble yourself in order to build a team. Humility allows you to see the need for others. Pride insists on working alone.

2. You cannot seek a position and have the team succeed. Following Jesus keeps you on mission and out of competition with others.

3. You must be willing to give up your personal right to be served and find greatness in service to the mission and the other team members.

4. You must trust that God is in control of your life in order to risk service to those on the team.

5. You must take up the towel of service to meet the needs of the group.

6. You must share both responsibility and authority with team members in order to meet the greater need of the team's goal.

7. You must multiply your leadership by empowering other members of the team to lead.[8]

— C. GENE WILKES
JESUS ON LEADERSHIP

THIS MUST BE THE PLACE

Every effective leader knows that you can win with good players. And you can lose with good players. But you cannot win without good players.

One of the things that separates winning and losing teams is how the team's good players are placed. Take a look at what I mean:

The Wrong Person in the Wrong Place   =   REGRESSION

The Wrong Person in the Right Place   =   FRUSTRATION

The Right Person in the Wrong Place   =   CONFUSION

The Right Person in the Right Place   =   PROGRESSION

The Right People in the Right Places   =   MULTIPLICATION

We should not only use all the brains

we have, but all that we can borrow.

— PRESIDENT
WOODROW WILSON

If we don't know it, we can't show it. Paul "Bear" Bryant, the legendary football coach at the University of Alabama, said that winning team members need to know five things.

Tell me what you expect from me.

Give me an opportunity to perform.

Let me know how I'm getting along.

Give me guidance where I need it.

Reward me according to my contribution.

Enlarging Others

Team leaders have to connect—
with their team and themselves. If they
don't know their team's strengths and
weaknesses, they can not hand off
responsibilities to the team. And if
they don't know their own strengths
and weaknesses, they will not
hand off responsibilities to the team.

—John C. Maxwell

I have long been profoundly convinced

that in the very nature of things,

employers and employees are partners,

not enemies; that their interests are

common, not opposed; that in the long run

the success of each is dependent

upon the success of the other.

—JOHN D. ROCKEFELLER, JR.

The first thing you do
is teach the person to feel that the vision
is very important and nearly impossible.
That draws out the drive in the winner.

— EDWIN LAND

T here is an interesting story about an English artist named William Wolcott who went to New York in 1924 to record his impressions of that great city. One morning he was visiting in the office of a former colleague when the urge to sketch came over him. Seeing some paper on his friend's desk, he asked, "May I have that?"

His friend answered, "That's not sketching paper. That's ordinary wrapping paper."

Not wanting to lose that spark of inspiration, Wolcott took the wrapping paper and said, "Nothing is ordinary if you know how to use it." On that ordinary paper Wolcott made two sketches. Later that same year, one of those sketches sold for $500 and the other for $1,000, quite a lot for 1924.

People under the influence of an empowering person are like paper in the hands of a great artist. No matter what they're made of, they can become treasures.

The ability to empower others is one of the keys to personal and professional success. John Craig said, "No matter how much work you can do, no matter how engaging your personality may be, you will not advance far in business if you cannot work through others." And business executive J. Paul Getty said, "It doesn't make much difference how much other knowledge or experience an executive possesses; if he is unable to achieve results through people, he is worthless as an executive."

— *Becoming a Person of Influence*

Success feeds on itself, not just by

attracting better talent to projects,

but by raising your own team's level of

confidence and passion for the project.

— MICHAEL EISNER

WORK IN PROGRESS

Over the years I've learned a lot about
coaching staffs and one piece of advice
I would pass on to a young coach —
or a corporation executive or even a
bank president — is this: Don't make
them in your image. Don't even try.
My assistants don't look alike,
think alike, or have the same personalities.
And I sure don't want them all thinking
the way I do. You don't strive for
sameness; you strive for balance.

— PAUL "BEAR" BRYANT

Every team leader desires players who will make significant contributions that take the team to the top. In sports, when a player steps up during crunch time, that individual is often recognized as the most valuable player.

The caliber of play comes from the caliber of the player. Any team player has the potential to be the MVP, as long as he or she . . .

Visualizes what can be, not just what is

Appreciates the other players

Leads by example

Understands the big picture

Adds value to the entire team

Brings home the bacon

Learns quickly from mistakes

Encourages others

To be trusted is a better compliment

than to be loved.

— GEORGE MACDONALD

Motivate employees, train them,
care about them, and make winners of them.
At Marriott we know that if we treat
our employees correctly, they'll treat
the customers right. And if the customers are
treated right, they'll come back.

— BILL MARRIOTT
CEO MARRIOTT HOTELS

The difference between a Tower of Babel
and a tower of strength is the difference
between those who live to make themselves
more and those who know the way
to heaven is in making others more.

— NOAH BEN SHEA
JACOB'S JOURNEY

I think most of us are looking for a calling,

not a job. Most of us, like the assembly line worker,

have jobs that are too small for our spirit.

Jobs are not big enough for people.

—STUDS TERKEL

WORKING

Contrary to popular myth, great teams are not characterized by an absence of conflict. On the contrary, in my experience, one of the most reliable indicators of a team that is continually learning is the visible conflict of ideas. In great teams conflict becomes productive. There may, and often will, be conflict around the vision. In fact, the essence of the "visioning" process lies in the gradual emergence of a shared vision from different personal visions. Even when people share a common vision, they have many different ideas about how to achieve that vision. The loftier the vision, the more uncertain we are how it is to be achieved. The free flow of conflicting ideas is critical for creative thinking, for discovering new solutions no one individual would have come to on his own. Conflict becomes, in effect, part of the ongoing dialogue.[9]

— PETER SENGE

THE FIFTH DISCIPLINE

What is Your Dream?

TO ACHIEVE ALL THAT IS POSSIBLE,
WE MUST ATTEMPT THE IMPOSSIBLE.
TO BE ALL WE CAN BE, WE MUST DREAM
OF BEING MORE. TO REACH OUR DREAMS,
WE MUST REACH OUT TO OTHERS.

—JOHN C. MAXWELL

The successful attainment of a dream
is a cart and horse affair.
Without a team of horses,
a cart full of dreams can go nowhere.

— REX MURPHY

Most men die from the neck up
at age twenty-five
because they stop dreaming.

— BEN FRANKLIN

One of the great dreamers of the twentieth century was Walt Disney. Any person who could create the first sound cartoon, first all-color cartoon, and first animated feature-length motion picture is definitely someone with vision. But Disney's greatest masterpieces of vision were Disneyland and Walt Disney World. And the spark for that vision came from an unexpected place.

Back when Walt's two daughters were young, he used to take them to an amusement park in the Los Angeles area on Saturday mornings. His girls loved it, and he did too. Amusement parks were a kid's paradise, with wonderful atmosphere: the smell of popcorn and cotton candy, the gaudy colors of signs advertising rides, and the sound of kids screaming as the roller coaster plummeted over a hill.

The carousel especially captivated Walt. As he approached it, he saw a blur of bright images racing around to the tune of energetic calliope music. But when he got closer and the carousel stopped, he could see that his eye had been fooled. What he observed was shabby horses with cracked and chipped paint. And he noticed that only the horses on the outside row moved up and down. The others stood lifeless, bolted to the floor.

The cartoonist's disappointment inspired him with a grand vision for an amusement park where the illusion didn't evaporate, where children and adults could enjoy a great carnival atmosphere without the seedy side that accompanies some circuses and traveling carnivals. His dream became Disneyland.

The seed for most people's dreams naturally springs from their everyday experiences. If you have not yet identified your dream, just keep your eyes and ears open, listen to your heart, and be open to every possibility.

— *THE 21 INDISPENSABLE QUALITIES OF A LEADER*

A goal properly set is halfway reached.

If you can dream it, you can do it.
Never lose sight of the fact that this
whole thing was started by a mouse.

— WALT DISNEY

People with goals succeed
because they know where they're going.

— EARL NIGHTINGALE

Teamwork requires that
everyone's efforts flow in a single direction.
Feelings of significance happen when
a team's energy takes on a life of its own.

— PAT RILEY
THE WINNER WITHIN

A common reason goals aren't accomplished
is they are not clearly defined. If employees
don't understand their company's goals and
its game plan, these goals won't be achieved.

Football doesn't make this mistake.
Its goals are always clearly defined.
At the end of the field is a goal line.

Why do we call it a goal line?
Because eleven people on the offensive
team huddle for a single purpose—
to move the ball across it. Everyone has
a specific task to do—the quarterback,
the wide receiver, each lineman, every player
knows exactly what his assignment is.
Even the defensive team has its goals, too—
to prevent the offensive team from
achieving its goal.

— JIM TUNNEY

Make no small plans for they have

no capacity to stir men's souls.

— Source Unknown

When Rick Hoyt was born in 1962, his parents possessed the typical excited expectations of first-time parents. But then they discovered that during Rick's birth, his umbilical cord had wrapped around his neck, cutting off the oxygen to his brain. Later, Rick was diagnosed with cerebral palsy. "When he was eight months old," his father, Dick, remembers, "the doctors told us we should put him away—he'd be a vegetable all his life." But Rick's parents wouldn't do that. They were determined to raise him like any other kid.

AN UPHILL BATTLE

Sometimes that was tough. Rick is a quadriplegic who cannot speak because he has limited control of his tongue. But Rick's parents worked with him, teaching him everything they could and including him in family activities. When Rick was ten, his life changed when engineers from Tufts University created a device that enabled him to communicate via computer. The first words he slowly and painstakingly punched out were, "Go Bruins." That's when the family, who had been following the NHL's Boston Bruins in the playoffs, found out Rick was a sports fan.

In 1975, after a long battle the family was finally able to get

Rick into public school, where he excelled despite his physical limitations. Rick's world was changing. It changed even more two years later. When Rick found out that a fund-raising five-kilometer race was being put on to help a young athlete who had been paralyzed in an accident, he told his father that he wanted to participate.

Dick, then a lieutenant colonel in the Air National Guard, was in his late thirties and out of shape. But he agreed to run and push his son in a modified wheelchair. When they crossed the finish line—second to last—Dick recalls, Rick flashed "the biggest smile you ever saw in your life." After the race, Rick wrote out this simple message: "Dad, I felt like I wasn't handicapped." After that day, their lives would never be the same again.

WORKING TOGETHER

What does a father do when his son, who has never been out of a wheelchair, says that he loves to race? He becomes his boy's hands and feet. That's the day "Team Hoyt" was born. Dick got Rick a more sophisticated racing chair. Then the quadriplegic teenager and the out-of-shape dad began running together—and not just casually. Before long, their training became more serious, and in 1981, they ran in their first Boston Marathon together. Since, then, they haven't missed a Boston Marathon in twenty years.

After four years of running marathons, the two decided that they were ready for another challenge: triathlons, events which combine swimming, cycling, and running. That was no small challenge, especially because Dick would have to learn how to swim! But he did. Dick explained, "He's the one who has motivated me because if it wasn't for him, I wouldn't be out there competing. What I'm doing is loaning Rick my arms and legs so he can be out there competing like everybody else."

Of all the races in the world, one is considered the toughest—the Ironman Triathlon in Hawaii. The race consists of three back-to-back legs: a 2.4-mile swim, a 112-mile bike race, and a full marathon run of 26.2 miles. It's an excruciating test of stamina for any individual. In 1989, Dick and Rick competed in the race together. For the swimming portion, Dick towed a small boat with Rick in it. Then he biked for the 112 miles with Rick in a seat on his bicycle's handlebars. By the time they got to the running leg, Dick was exhausted.

But all Dick had to do was think of the words of his son:

> When I'm running, my disability seems to disappear. It is the only place where truly I feel as an equal. Due to all the positive feedback, I do not feel handicapped at all. Rather, I feel that I am the intelligent person that I am with no limits.

And of course, they finished the race—in a strong time of thirteen hours and forty-three minutes. Since then, Rick has earned his college degree, and he works at Boston University helping to design computer systems for people with disabilities. And of course, he still competes with his father, who is now over 60 years old and retired. As of March 2001, Team Hoyt had completed a total of 731 races. They've run 53 marathons and 135 triathlons, including four races at Ironman distances. And they will keep running. "There is nothing in the world that the both of us can't conquer together," says Dick. They live out the truth that a dream—and a team—can take you anywhere.[10]

— THE 17 INDISPUTABLE LAWS OF TEAMWORK

Walt Disney never let
practical realities get in the way
of his imagination.
"It's my job to dream the dreams,"
he once said, chuckling.
"But paying for 'em?
That's my brother Roy's job."

I f you lead a team, then you need a dream. If you have a dream, then you need a team. One will not succeed without the other. So as you lead, heed the advice of my friend Florence Littauer:

Dare to Dream . . .

Have the desire to do something bigger than yourself

Prepare the Dream . . .

Do your homework; be ready when the opportunity comes.

Wear the Dream . . .

Do it!

Share the Dream . . .

Make others a part of the dream, and it will become even greater than you had hoped.

So, how dedicated are you to your dream? Are you content just to dream it or are you willing to take the risk and try to live it? If you're ready to turn your dream into reality, here is how to get started:

1. Make the Decision to Build a Team

Every action begins with a decision. Teams don't just build themselves. If you want to see your dream come to fruition, dedicate yourself to team building. Take care of the team, and it will take care of the dream.

2. Gather the Best Players Possible

The better the players on the team, the greater the team's potential for success. The bigger the dream, the better the team you need. Start well, and the rest of the process is a lot easier.

3. Pay the Price to Develop the Team

Team building has a price, in energy, money, and time. When you build a team, you pay with your life. But if you do, in return you receive a better life.

4. Do Things Together as a Team

Good team leaders know that you touch a heart before you ask for a hand. That's the Law of Connection. The way you create that connection is by doing things together.

5. Empower Team Members with Responsibility and Authority

A team can achieve only when its individual members are vested with responsibility and authority. Responsibility gives them the desire. Authority gives them the means. Empowered team members achieve more and help the team to continually improve.

6. Give Credit for Success to the Team

Too many leaders steal their team's ego food. If you want your team to keep fighting for the dream, then remember that nothing motivates a team like recognition. Put the credit where it belongs—with the people who get the job done.

7. Watch to See That the Investment in the Team Is Paying Off

As a team leader, you can never afford to stop investing in your people. Everyone doesn't naturally grow on his own. However, activity does not always mean accomplishment. You need to measure your investment. Be sure that you're doing the right things to help your people. You can do that by paying attention to what's paying off.

8. Stop Investing in Players Who Do Not Grow

It's sad to say, but not every investment in people pays off. When that happens, you must stop giving your best attention to those who aren't growing. Life is short, and for every person who won't or can't grow, there is someone else who would love to benefit from what you have to give.

9. Create New Opportunities for the Team

One of the roles of team leaders is to help the team to succeed. That means finding new opportunities for the team. No matter how long your team has been together or how successful you have been in the past, never let a day go by that you're not looking for ways to help your team keep moving forward.

10. Give the Team the Best Possible Chance to Succeed

In the end, the team fails or succeeds together. The best way to serve the individuals on the team is to see that the whole team wins. Do that, and dreams can come true for everyone.

Keep your goals out of reach,

but not out of sight.

— AUTHOR UNKNOWN

1. "Mount Everest History/Facts." <http://www.mnteverest.com/history.html> 10 December 2001.

2. Ullman, James Ramsey. *Man of Everest: The Autobiography of Tenzing.* London: George G. Harrap and Co., Ltd., 1955, 178.

3. Ibid, 255.

4. "Passers-By Aid in Rescue," *Los Angeles Times*, 20 November 1988.

5. Graham, Billy. *Just As I Am: The Autobiography of Billy Graham*. San Francisco: Harper Collins, 1997, p. 662.

6; "Life Together," *Christianity Today*, 9 July 2001, p. 26.

7. "History of the Mayo Clinic." Mayo Clinic. <http://www.mayoclinic.org/about/history.html> 8 October 2001.

8. Wilkes, Gene. *Jesus on Leadership*. Wheaton, IL: Tyndale House Publishers, 1998, p. 212.

9. Senge, Peter. *The Fifth Discipline*. New York: Currency/Doubleday, 1994, p. 249.

10. Tereshchuk, David, "Racing Toward Inclusion." <http://www.teamhoyt.com/history.shtml> 14 March 2001.